MOTIVATION 365
OVERCOMING GRIEF AND LOSS

Quotes, Lyrics, Proverbs, Poems, Psalms and Prayers

Inspiring your Recovery, Well-Being and Happiness - Every day of the Year.

S.D. HARRAZIE

Copyright © 2020 by Saul Daniel Harrazie

All rights reserved. This book or any portion thereof may not be reproduced or used in any manner whatsoever without the express written permission of the publisher except for the use of brief quotations in a book review.

Printed in the United Kingdom

First Printing, 2020

ISBN: 9798639165061

CONTENTS

Introduction 1

Making This Book Work For You 4

365 Days Of Motivational Quotes 6

Afterword 114

Introduction

Its a sad fact that over our lifetimes many of our favourite people will come into our lives, giving us love, affection, generosity, perhaps someone you always look forward to seeing. Then for a variety of reasons the relationship ends. Your life has changed forever, whilst the World around you goes on as normal. Yet you feel that your World has collapsed, the person who has left you has left an indelible mark in your heart and an imprint on your mind. People can grieve over different types of losses, for example: loss of a job, news of a terminal illness, divorce, death of a partner or child, loss of financial security or a death of a pet.

Just as sure as there are beginnings to ambition, relationships and life, there are also endings to these. Since the beginning of civilisation, everyday people appear and disappear, Empires crumble into dust and new ones are created. Nobody can outrun, "Father Time". Your happiness in life is inextricably linked with how you deal with these inevitable endings.

Everybody deals with grief and loss in different ways, each loss is unique and personal to each individual, there are no right or wrong way of dealing with this. There's no time limits on how long you will feel the raw pain of a loss, you may have lost a relationship that is quite simply irreplaceable, besides something's in life were not meant to be replaced.

The fundamental idea of this book is to endeavour to get the reader to accept their loss. Once a loss is accepted the route to a more joyous and happy life will be tha much closer. This book is a self-help book and aims to use engaging words of wisdom, some humour, verses, prayers and songs etc, **to unlock the readers power of positive-thinking.** People of all Religions and non-religious people can equally reap the benefits of reading this book.

Before you start your journey to acceptance it is noteworthy that some of the authors specifically state a particular religion, its entirely up to the reader to decide if a quote is applicable to themselves or not. On a personal note - in terms of Religion I'd like to believe there are many roads to the same destination.

Readers will benefit with understanding the Kubler Ross Model of The Five Stages of Grief before they go any further: This model of Grief and recovery was first pioneered by psychologist Elizabeth Kubler Ross in 1969. This is probably the best known model of the grieving process.

The Five Stages of Grief

Denial:

This cannot happen to me!

Anger:

Why did this happen to me? Who's to blame for this?

Bargaining:

Please God just let them/me live 'til my sons wedding, and I'll do anything.

Depression:

I am too sad to do anything.

Acceptance:

I'm at peace and accept it, I can plan for the future.

Making This Book Work for You

This book has been designed to work for you, in a variety of ways

A. You can choose to start from quote number 1 in numerical order to quote Number 365. As this book is Motivation 365, it has a quote for every day of the year. Readers should remember each daily quote or even write it down and look at it a few times during the day. This will help you keep the faith and give you hope.

B. Essentially this book can be used by people who might be grieving or feeling the effects of a loss. Simply leave it in a place where it might be picked up. Remember this is a Self-Help book and places an onus on the reader to tap into their own self-belief to unlock positive feelings and thoughts.

C. You can opt to read this book in one, from cover to cover or from the beginning to the end. *It is noteworthy that some of the verses and contributions contained in this book, might cause the reader to become emotional. If at any-time you feel over-*

whelmed by a contribution -just skip the particular passage or perhaps revisit it on another occasion.

D. Alternatively just randomly select a number each day, from number 1 to number 365. Then read the corresponding quote to help inspire your day ahead

E. Reach for this book any time you are feeling down - nobody knows when grief and loss will visit them. You might want to use a verse to comfort a friends or relative during challenging times.

365 Days of Motivational Quotes

(Overcoming Grief and Pain)

1.

He will wipe every tear from their eyes. There will be no more death' or mourning or crying or pain, for old order of things has passed away.

(Revelation 21: 4)

2.

We should feel sorrow but not sink under its oppression.

(Confucius)

3.

Cheers to my ex for finally finding someone just as worthless as he is.

(Unknown)

4.

Faith is taking the first step even when you don't see the whole staircase.

(Martin Luther King Jr)

5.

You "lost" your job. I don't think so. You know where that job is.

Think of it as the universe telling you it is time to "find" something better. Trust divine order.

(Mary Francis Winters)

6.

Someone once said to me, "Reverend Schuller, I hope you live to see all your dreams fulfilled." I replied, "I hope not, because if I live and all my dreams are fulfilled, I'm dead." It is unfulfilled dreams that keep you alive.

(Robert Schuller)

7.

Healing yourself is connected with healing others.

(Yoko Ono)

8.

Moving on, is a simple thing, what it leaves behind is hard.

(Dave Mustaine)

9.

Breaking up is a natural evolution when you try to figure out what you want in life. If you're with an individual who isn't moving in the same direction and at the same rate that you are, it ain't going to work.

(Usher)

10.

I've seen enough things to know that if you just keep on going, if you turn the corner, the sun will be shining.

(Reverend Al Sharpton)

11.

The most important thing is to enjoy your life - to be happy - it's all that matters.

(Audrey Hepburn)

12.

Remember that everyone you meet is afraid of something, loves something, and has lost something.

(H.Jackson Brown Jr)

13.

It's kinda hard with you not around (yeah)
Know you in heaven smilin' down
Watchin' us while we pray for you
Every day we pray for you
Till the day we meet again
In my heart is where I'll keep you friend
Memories give me the strength I need (uh-huh) to proceed
Strength I need to believe
My thoughts big I just can't define (can't define)
Wish I could turn back the hands of time.

(I'll be Missing You - Puff Daddy/Faith Evans)

14.

If the people we love are stolen from us, the way to have them live on is to never stop loving them.

(James O'Barr)

15.

Sometimes we lose friends for whose loss our regret is greater than our grief, and others for whom our grief is greater than our regret.

(Francois de la Rochefoucauld)

16.

Shattered dreams are never random. They are always a piece in a larger puzzle, a chapter in a larger story. The Holy Spirit uses the pain of shattered dreams to help us discover our desire for God, to help us begin dreaming the highest dream. They are ordained opportunities for the Spirit to awaken, then to satisfy our highest dream.

(Larry Crabb)

17.

Your dream doesn't have an expiration date. Take a deep breath and try again.

(KT Witten)

18.

Lord, my heart is broken but You are near. My spirit is crushed, but You are my rescuer. Your Word is my hope. It revives me and comforts me   especially now. My soul faints, but you are the breath of life within me. You are my help, the One who sustains me. I am weak but You are strong. You bless those who mourn, and I trust You to bless me and my family with all that we need. You will rescue me from this dark cloud of despair because You delight in me. In Jesus' Name, Amen.

(Jennifer White - Prayer for the Broken Hearted)

19.

Fake friends are like shadows: always near you at your brightest moments, but nowhere to be seen at your darkest hour True friends are like stars, you don't always see them but they are always there.

(Habeeb Akande)

20.

Where you used to be, there is a hole, which I find myself constantly walking around in the daytime, and falling in at night. I miss you like hell.

(Edna St. Vincent Millay)

21.

I learned more stuff in church than I did in the world.

(Al Green)

22.

Today I choose life. Every morning when I wake up I can choose joy, happiness, negativity, pain... To feel the freedom that comes from being able to continue to make mistakes and choices - today I choose to feel life, not to deny my humanity but embrace it.

(Kevyn Aucoin)

23.

Some memories are unforgettable, remaining ever vivid and heartwarming!

(Joseph B Wirthlin)

24.

To live in hearts we leave behind is not to die.

(Thomas Campbell)

25.

He heals the brokenhearted and binds up their wounds.

(Psalm 147:3)

26.

You must make a decision that you are going to move on. It wont happen automatically. You will have to rise up and say, 'I don't care how hard this is, I don't care how disappointed I am, I'm not going to let this get the best of me. I'm moving on with my life.

(Joel Osteen)

27.

Don't cry because its over
Smile Because it happened

(Dr Seuss)

28.

Friendship... is not something you learn in school. But if you haven't learned the meaning of friendship, you really haven't learned anything.

(Muhammad Ali)

29.

The Comfort Prayer

Jesus, You said, "Blessed are those who mourn, for they will be comforted" . I am mourning; send me Your comfort now. Wrap around Your arms around me and hold me tight. Send angels of mercy to me. Shower Your comfort on me through those around me, and keep far from me those whose words and actions are no comfort. Amen.

(Matthew 5:4)

30.

Life does not cease to be funny when people die anymore than it ceases to be serious when people laugh.

(George Bernard Shaw)

31.

The flower fades and dies, but he who wears the flower has not to mourn for it for ever.

(Rabindranath Tagore)

32.

Gratitude changes the pangs of memory into a tranquil joy.

(Dietrich Bonhoeffer)

33.

(Do Not Stand at my Grave and Weep)

Do not stand at my grave and weep
I am not there; I do not sleep.
I am a thousand winds that blow,
I am the diamond glints on snow,
I am the sun on ripened grain,
I am the gentle autumn rain.
When you awaken in the morning's hush
I am the swift uplifting rush
Of quiet birds in circled flight.
I am the soft stars that shine at night.
Do not stand at my grave and cry,
I am not there; I did not die.

(Poem by Mary Elizabeth Fraye)

34.

A believer smiles in public and weeps in private.

(Abu Maryam)

35.

Don't be in a hurry to condemn because he doesn't do what you do or think as you think or as fast. There was a time when you didn't know what you know today.

(Malcolm X)

36.

Grief can be a burden, but also an anchor. You can get used to the weight, how it holds you in place.

(Sarah Dessen)

37.

Pain is a reality, suffering is a choice.

(Rabbi Asher Resnick)

38.

Don't brood. Get on with living and loving. You don't have forever.

(Leo Buscaglia)

39.

Every atom in Your body came from a star that exploded. And, the atoms in your left hand probably came from a different star than your right hand. It really is the most poetic thing I know about physics: You are all stardust. You couldn't be here if stars hadn't exploded, because the elements - the carbon, nitrogen, oxygen, iron, all the things that matter for evolution - weren't created at the beginning of time. They were created in the nuclear furnaces of stars. So, forget Jesus. The stars died so that You could be here today.

(Lawrence M. Krauss)

40.

The way I see it, if you want the rainbow

you gotta put up with the rain.

(Dolly Parton)

41.

Often when you think you're at the end of something, you're at the beginning of something else.

(Fred Rogers)

42.

Four Feet

I have done mostly what most men do,
And pushed it out of my mind;
But I can't forget, if I wanted to,
Four-Feet trotting behind.

Day after day, the whole day through --
Wherever my road inclined --
Four-feet said, "I am coming with you!"
And trotted along behind.

Now I must go by some other round, --
Which I shall never find --
Somewhere that does not carry the sound
Of Four-Feet trotting behind.

(Rudyard Kipling)

43.

At times our own light goes out and is rekindled by a spark from another person. Each of us has cause to think with deep gratitude of those who have lighted the flame within us.

(Albert Schweitzer)

44.

You will be Missed

Saying goodbye
Was the hardest thing to do.
I never thought I would,
Especially not to you.

You always listened
And knew what to say,
Knew when to give a hug
When I was having a bad day.

No one will ever take your place.
I can always promise you this.
It's hard to find someone like you,
So know you'll always be missed.

(Poem by Hanae Meloul)

45.

I'm prepared to meet my maker. Whether my maker is prepared for the ordeal of meeting me is another matter.

(Winston Churchill)

46.

Eternity is a terrible thought. I mean,
where's it going to end?

(Tom Stoppard)

47.

My father said
Don't you worry, don't you worry child
See heaven's got a plan for you
Don't you worry, don't you worry now, yeah.

(Swedish House Mafia - Don't you Worry Child)

48.

Remember, hope is a good thing, maybe the best of
things, and no good thing ever dies.

(Stephen King)

49.

If tears could build a stairway,
And memories a lane,
I'd walk right up to Heaven
And bring you home again.

(Unknown)

50.

A sunrise and a sunset reminds us of new beginnings and a hope of a better tomorrow.

(Robert Krawczyk)

51.

We'll Meet Again

Lets say goodbye with a smile dear,
Just for a while dear we must part,
Don't let our parting upset you,
I'll no forget you sweetheart.

We'll meet again don't know where don't know when,
But I know we'll meet again some sunny day
Keep smiling through just as you always do.

(Dame Vera Lynn)

52.

When people walk away from you, let them go. Your destiny is never tied to anyone who leaves you, and it doesn't mean they are bad people. It just means that their part in your story is over.

(T.D Jakes)

53.

When those you love die, the best you can do is honor their spirit for as long as you live. You make a commitment that you're going to take whatever lesson that person or animal was trying to teach you, and you make it true in your own life. It's a positive way to keep their spirit alive in the world by keeping it alive in yourself.

(Patrick Swayze)

54.

We must be willing to let go of the life we have planned, so as to have the life that is waiting for us.

(E.M Forster)

55.

The world breaks everyone, and afterward, some are strong at the broken places.

(Ernest Hemingway)

56.

And ever has it been known that love knows not its own depth until the hour of separation.

(Khalil Gibran)

57.

JEHOVAH is "the God who gives hope, even amid sorrow.

(Romans 15:13)

58.

I want to be cremated
I know how boring funerals can be
I want people to gather
meet new people
have a laugh, a dance, meet a loved one.

(Sean Hughes)

59.

It happens to everyone as they grow up. You find out who you are and what you want, and then you realize that people you've known forever don't see things the way you do. So you keep the wonderful memories, but find yourself moving on.

(Nicholas Sparks)

60.

Divorce isn't such a tragedy. A tragedy's staying in an unhappy marriage, teaching your children the wrong things about love. Nobody ever died of divorce.

(Jennifer Weiner)

61.

Heavy hearts, like heavy clouds in the sky, are best relieved by the letting of a little water.

(Christopher Morley)

62.

Our sweetest songs are those that tell of saddest thought.

(Percy Bysshe Shelley)

63.

Many of them, like him, would never grow old enough to understand that you only go from one hardship to another. And that the best we can hope from life is that it is a wonderful depression.

(Heather O' Neil)

64.

The Way We Were

Memories light the corners of my mind
Misty water-colored memories of the way we were
Scattered pictures of the smiles we left behind
Smiles we gave to one another for the way we were

Can it be that it was all so simple then
Or has time rewritten every line
And if we had the chance to do it all again
Just tell me, tell me, would we, would we?
Could we, could we?

Memories may be beautiful and yet
So many memories too painful to remember
The way we were

(Barbra Streisand, Lionel Richie)

65.

I to die, and you to live. Which is better God only knows.

(Plato)

66.

Forgiveness is the fragrance that the violet sheds on the heel that has crushed it.

(Mark Twain)

67.

Indeed, with every hardship is ease.

(Quran 94: 6)

68.

I read and walked for miles... I read and walked for miles at night along the beach, writing bad blank verse and searching endlessly for someone wonderful who would step out of the darkness and change my life. It never crossed my mind that that person could be me.

(Anna Quindlen)

69.

Instead of mourning their death, celebrate their life.

(Marshall Bruce Mathers III)

70.

Perhaps they are not stars, but rather openings in heaven where the love of our lost ones pours through and shines down upon us to let us know they are happy.

(Eskimo Proverb)

71.

Wishing on a Star

I'm wishing on a star
To follow where you are
I'm wishing on a dream
To follow what it means

And I wish on all the rainbows that I see
I wish on all the people who really dream
And I'm wishing on tomorrow, praying it'll come
And I'm wishing on all the lovin' we've ever done.

(Rolls Royce)

72.

The day which we fear as our last is but the birthday of eternity.

(Seneca)

73.

Indecision, doubt and fear. The members of this unholy trio are closely related: where one is found, the others are close at hand.

(Napolean Hill)

74.

Love doesn't need to last a lifetime for it to be real. You can't judge the quality of a love by the length of time it lasts. Everything dies, love included. Sometimes it dies with a person, sometimes it dies on its own. The greatest love story ever told doesn't have to be about two people who spent their whole lives together. It might be about a love that lasted two weeks or two months or two years, but burned brighter and hotter and more brilliantly than any other love before or after. Don't mourn a failed love; there is no such thing. All love is equal in the brain.

(Krystal Sutherland, Our Chemical Hearts)

75.

Jesus said to her, "I am the resurrection and the life.[a] Whoever believes in me, though he die, yet shall he live, and everyone who lives and believes in me shall never die. Do you believe this?

(John 11:25 -26)

76.

I believe that imagination is stronger than knowledge. That myth is more potent than history. That dreams are more powerful than facts. That hope always triumphs over experience. That laughter is the only cure for grief. And I believe that love is stronger than death.

(Robert Fulghum)

77.

Those who are merciful will be shown mercy, by the Most Merciful. Be merciful to those on earth and the One in heaven will have mercy upon you.

(The Profit Muhammad)

78.

Sometimes good things fall apart so better things can fall together.

(Marilyn Monroe)

79.

If you don't love yourself, how in the hell you gonna love somebody else?

(RuPaul)

80.

God never said that the journey would be easy, but He did say that the arrival would be worthwhile.

(Max Lucado)

81.

Soldier

I was that which others did not want to be.
I went where others feared to go
and did what others failed to do.

I asked nothing from those who gave nothing,
and reluctantly accepted the thought of eternal loneliness... should I fail.

I have seen the face of terror; felt the stinging cold of fear;
and enjoyed the sweet taste of a moment's love.

I have cried, pained, and hoped... but most of all,
I have lived times others would say were best forgotten.

At Least someday I will be able to say
that I was proud of what I was... a Soldier.

(Poem, George L Skypeck)

82.

Wake up! If you knew for certain you had a terminal illness--if you had little time left to live--you would waste precious little of it! Well, I'm telling you...you do have a terminal illness: It's called birth. You don't have more than a few years left. No one does! So be happy now, without reason--or you will never be at all.

(Dan Millman)

83.

An angel in the book of life wrote down my baby's birth. Then whispered as she closed the book 'too beautiful for earth.

(Unknown)

84.

God turns clouds inside out to make fluffy beds for the dogs in Dog Heaven, and when they are tired from running and barking and eating ham-sandwich biscuits, the dogs find a cloud bed for sleeping. God watches over each one of them. And there are no bad dreams.

(Cynthia Rylant)

85.

It's funny how most people love the dead, once you're dead your made for life

(Jimi Hendrix)

86.

I've always believed that you shouldn't want to mend a broken heart, because that's someone you don't want to forget.

Scars can be good

(Joseph Fiennes)

87.

Death is nothing at all

I have only slipped away into the next room.
Whatever we were to each other, we still are.
Please, call me by my old familiar name.
Speak of me in the same easy way you always did.
Laugh, as we always laughed, at the little jokes we shared together.
Think of me and smile.

Let my name be the household name it always was,
Spoken without the shadow of a ghost in it.
Life means all it ever meant.
It is the same as it ever was.
Death is inevitable, so why should I be out of mind because I am out of sight?

I am but waiting for you, - for an interval very near.
Nothing is past or lost.
One brief moment and all will be as it was before,
Only better and happier.
Together forever.
All is well.

(Poem by Henry Scott Holland)

88.

Change is the Law of the Universe

What you have taken, Has been from here
What you gave has been given here
What belongs to you today
belonged to someone yesterday
and will be someone else's tomorrow
Change is the Law of The Universe

(The Bhagavad Gita - Hindu Scriptures)

89.

Jesus has been in my room. He has taken my hand and told me, No, Not now. I have other things for you to do.

(Patsy Cline)

90.

We write our names in the sand: and then the waves roll in and wash them away.

(Augustus)

91.

What soap is for the body, tears are for the soul.

(Jewish Proverb)

92.

The 3 C's in life: Choice, Chance, Change. You must make the choice, take the chance, if you want anything in life to change.

(Unknown)

93.

The moment I wake up

Before I put on my makeup

I say a little prayer for you.

(Aretha Franklin)

94.

Be assured that just as an hour is only part of a day, so life on Earth is only part of eternity.

(C.L. Allen)

95.

Where there is no struggle, there is no strength.

(Oprah Winfrey)

96.

Healing takes courage, and we all have courage, even if we have to dig a little to find it

(Tori Amos)

97.

Even in darkness, it is possible to create light.

(Elie Wiesel)

98.

Truth is everybody is going to hurt you: you just gotta find the ones worth suffering for.

(Bob Marley)

99.

Forgiveness says you are given another chance to make a new beginning.

(Desmond Tutu)

100.

Never Dreamed You'd Leave In the Summer

I never dreamed you'd leave in summer
I thought you would go then come back home
I thought the cold would leave by summer
But my quiet nights will be spent alone

You said there would be warm love in springtime
That is when you started to be cold
I never dreamed you'd leave in summer
But now I find myself all alone

You said then you'd be the life in autumn
Said you'd be the one to see the way
No I never dreamed you'd leave in summer
But now I find my love has gone away

Why didn't you stay?

(Stevie Wonder)

101.

The stars are a free show; it don't cost anything to use your eyes.

(Eric Arthur Blair)

102.

And know that I am with you always; yes, to the end of time.

(Jesus Christ)

103.

If I had my life to live over again, I would have made a rule to read some poetry and listen to some music at least once every week.

(Charles Darwin)

104.

Know the world in yourself. Never look for yourself in the world, for this would be to project your illusion.

(Egyptian Proverb)

105.

When in the eyes of the beloved riches count not, gold and dust are as one to thee.

(Saadi Shirazi)

106.

Let Me Go

When I come to the end of the road
And the sun has set for me
I want no rites in a gloom filled room
Why cry for a soul set free?

Miss me a little, but not for long
And not with your head bowed low
Remember the love that once we shared
Miss me, but let me go.

For this is a journey we all must take
And each must go alone.
It's all part of the master plan
A step on the road to home.

When you are lonely and sick at heart
Go to the friends we know.
Laugh at all the things we used to do
Miss me, but let me go.

(Poem by Christina Rosetti)

107.

Lost time is never found again.

(Benjamin Franklin)

108.

All the world will be your enemy, Prince with a Thousand Enemies, and whenever they catch you, they will kill you. But first they must catch you, digger, listener, runner, prince with the swift warning. Be cunning and full of tricks and your people shall never be destroyed.

(Richard Adams -Watership Down)

109.

Have you no wish for others to be saved? Then you are not saved yourself.

(Charles Spurgeon)

110.

Things are beautiful if you love them.

(Jean Anouilh)

111.

One thing I ask from the LORD, this only do I seek: that I may dwell in the house of the LORD all the days of my life, to gaze on the beauty of the LORD and to seek him in his temple.

(Psalm 27:4)

112.

If you spend your time hoping someone will suffer the consequences for what they did to your heart, then you're allowing them to hurt second time in your mind.

(Shannon L Adler)

113.

So long as the memory of certain beloved friends lives in my heart, I shall say that life is good.

(Helen Keller)

114.

The saddest thing about betrayal is that it never comes from your enemies, it comes from those you trust the most

(xxxtentacion)

115.

I never saw a wild thing sorry for itself. A small bird will drop frozen dead from a bough without ever having felt sorry for itself.

(D.H Lawrence)

116.

In any moment of decision the best thing you can do is the right thing, the next best thing is the wrong thing. and the worst thing you can do is nothing.

(Theodore Roosevelt)

117.

Heavy misfortunes have befallen us, but let us only cling to what remains, and transfer our love for those whom we have lost to those who yet live.

(Mary Shelley)

118.

By being yourself, you put something wonderful in the world that was not there before.

(Edwin Elliot)

119.

Anything in life that we don't accept will simply make trouble for us until we make peace with it.

(Shakti Gawain)

120.

Speak when you are angry - and you'll make the best speech   you'll ever regret.

(Laurence J. Peter)

121.

Miracles are not contrary to nature, but only contrary to what we know about nature.

(Saint Augustine)

122.

If I must die,

I will encounter darkness as a bride,

And hug it in mine arms

(William Shakespeare - Measure for Measure)

123.

We must embrace pain and burn it as fuel for our journey.

(Kenji Miyazawa)

124.

Amazing Grace

Amazing Grace

Amazing Grace! How sweet the sound
That saved a wretch like me!
I once was lost, but now am found
Was blind, but now I see.

'Twas Grace that taught my heart to fear,
And Grace my fears relieved.
How precious did that Grace appear
The hour I first believed.

Through many dangers, toils, and snares
I have already come.
'Tis Grace hath brought me safe thus far
And Grace will lead me home.

The Lord has promised good to me.
His Word my hope secures.
He will my shield and portion be
As long as life endures.

When we've been there ten thousand years
Bright shining as the sun,
We've no less days to sing God's praise
Than when we'd first begun.

(John Newton)

125.

Everyone of us needs to show how much we care for each other and, in the process, care for ourselves.

(Princess Diana)

126.

We must be willing to let go of the life we have planned, so as to accept the life that is waiting for us.

(Joseph Campbell)

127.

Some cause happiness wherever they go; others whenever they go.

(Oscar Wilde)

128.

In the depth of winter, I finally learned that within me there lay an invincible summer.

(Albert Camus)

129.

Let go.   Why do you cling to pain?   There is nothing you can do about the wrongs of yesterday.   It is not yours to judge.   Why hold on to the very thing which keeps you from hope and love?

(Leo Buscaglia)

130.

This is the day the Lord made;

we shall rejoice and be glad.

(Psalm 118:24)

131.

I intend to live forever, or die trying.

(Groucho Marx)

132.

Even though the future seems far away, it is actually beginning right now.

(Mattie Stepanek)

133.

Disturb us Lord

When we are too pleased with ourselves,
When our dreams have come true
Because we dreamed too little,
When we arrived safely
Because we sailed too close to the shore.

Disturb us Lord,
When with the abundance of things we possess
We have lost our thirst for the waters of life;
Having fallen in love with life,
We have ceased to dream of eternity
And in our efforts to build a new earth,
We have allowed our vision of the new Heaven to dim.

Disturb us Lord,
To dare more boldly,
To venture on wilder seas,
Where storms will show Your mastery;
Where losing sight of land,
We shall find the stars.

We ask you to push back
The horizons of our hopes;
And to push back the future
In strength, courage, hope, and love.

(Sir Francis Drake)

134.

When the rain is blowing in your face
And the whole world is on your case
I could offer you a warm embrace
To make you feel my love.

(Bob Dylan)

135.

I've been heartbroken. I've broken hearts. That's part of life, and its part of figuring out who you are so you can find the right partner.

(Heidi Klum)

136.

Sometimes in our lives we all have pain
We all have sorrow
But if we are wise
We know that there's always tomorrow

Lean on me, when you're not strong
And I'll be your friend
I'll help you carry on
For it won't be long
'Til I'm gonna need
Somebody to lean on

(Bill Withers - Lean on Me)

137.

It's a source of great sadness to me that my father died without having seen me do anything worthwhile. He was constantly having to make excuses for me.

(Daniel Day-Lewis)

138.

A boy said to a man "I want happiness." The man said "Remove 'I' - that is your ego. Remove 'want' - that is your desire. And what remains is your happiness."

(Yasmin Mogahed)

139.

You see things and you say, 'Why?'. But I dream things and I say, 'Why not?'.

(George Bernard Shaw)

140.

Is He (not best) who responds to the desperate one when he calls upon Him and removes evil and makes you inheritors of the earth.

Is there deity with Allah? Little do you remember.

(The Quran 27:62)

141.

Whatever you want to do, do it now. There are only so many tomorrows.

(Michael Landon)

142.

Sometimes blessings are not what God gives, but what he takes away.

Blessings in disguise.

(Unknown)

143.

Your friend is your needs answered.

(Khalil Gibran)

144.

Death leaves a heartache no one can heal, love leaves a memory no one can steal.

(Richard Puz)

145.

A Prayer For Animals

Hear our humble prayer,
O God,
for our friends, the animals,
especially for those who are suffering;
for any that are lost or deserted
or frightened or hungry.

We entreat for them all
Thy mercy and pity,
and for those who deal with them,
we ask a heart of compassion
and gentle hands and kindly words.

Make us, ourselves,
to be true friends to animals
and so to share
the blessings
of the merciful.

(Albert Schweitzer)

146.

Cancer can take away all of my physical abilities. It cannot touch my mind, it cannot touch my heart, and it cannot touch my soul.

(Jim Valvano)

147.

The truest end of life, is to know the life that never ends.

For death is no more than a turning of us over from time to eternity. Death, then, being the way and condition of life, we cannot love to live, if we cannot bear to die.

They that love beyond the world cannot be separated by it. Death cannot kill what never dies. Nor can spirits ever be divided that love and live in the same Divine Principle, the root and record of their friendship.

If absence be not death, neither is theirs.

Death is but crossing the world, as friends do the seas; they live in one another still.

(William Penn)

148.

May laughter fill your home, relieve your stress, and strengthen your friendships. Do not let a day go buy without laughing; it is good for your health.

(Catherine Pulsifer)

149.

Forgiveness is the final form of love.

(Reinhold Niebuhr)

150.

My entire life has been inspired by how my family has made me feel.

(Michael Buble)

151.

There are three of you. There is the person you think you are. There is the person others think you are. There is the person God knows you are and can be through Christ.

(Billy Graham)

152.

Life is short, Break the Rules. Forgive quickly, Kiss slowly. Love truly. Laugh uncontrollably And never regret ANYTHING That makes you smile.

(Mark Twain)

153.

Faith is the bird that feels the light when the dawn is still dark. **(Rabindranath Tagore)**

154.

Letting go doesn't mean that you don't care about someone anymore.

Its just realising that the only person you really have control over is yourself.

(Deborah Reber)

155.

Can miles truly separate you from friends, If you want to be with someone you love, aren't you already there?

(Richard Bach)

156.

Tension is who you think you should be. Relaxation is who you are.

(Chinese Proverb)

157.

Sometimes, when one person is missing, the whole world seems depopulated.

(Lamartine)

158.

Instead of getting married again, I'm going to find a woman I don't like and give her a house.

(Lewis Grizzard)

159.

Grief is never something you get over. You don't wake up one morning and say, 'I've conquered that; now I'm moving on.' It's something that walks beside you every day. And if you can learn how to manage it and honour the person that you miss, you can take something that is incredibly sad and have some form of positivity.

(Terri Irwin)

160.

Saving us is the greatest and most concrete demonstration of God's love, the definitive display of His grace throughout time and eternity.

(David Jeremaih)

161.

I can't change the direction of the wind, but I can adjust my sails to always reach my destination.

(Jimmy Dean)

162.

Bridge Over Troubled Waters

When you're weary, feeling small
When tears are in your eyes
I will dry them all
I'm on your side
Oh when times get rough
And friends just can't be found

Like a bridge over troubled water
I will lay me down
Like a bridge over troubled water
I will lay me down

When you're down and out
When you're on the street
When evening falls so hard
I will comfort you
I'll take your part
Oh when darkness comes
And pain is all around

Like a bridge over troubled water
I will lay me down
Like a bridge over troubled water
I will lay me down.

(Simon and Garfunfel)

163.

As a well spent day brings happy sleep, so life well used brings happy death.

(Leonardo da Vinci)

164.

I say I am stronger than fear.

(Malala Yousafzai)

165.

A failed relationship is just a stepping stone to a perfect ending.

(Ginger Smith)

166.

Everything you want is on the other side of fear.

(Jack Canfield)

167.

Don't bury your failures, let them inspire you.

(Robert Kiyosaki)

168.

The risk of love is loss, and the price of loss is grief. But the pain of grief is only a shadow when compared with the pain of never risking love.

(Hilary Stanton Zunin)

169.

No evil shall befall you, nor shall affliction come near your tent, for His Angels God has given command about you, that they guard you in all your ways.

(Psalm 91:10)

170.

What, if some day or night a demon were to steal after you into your loneliest loneliness and say to you: 'This life as you now live it and have lived it, you will have to live once more and innumerable times more.

(Friedrich Nietzsche)

171.

Apache Blessing

May the sun
Bring you new energy by day,
May the moon
Softly restore you by night,
May the rain
Wash away your worries,
May the breeze
Blow new strength into your being,
May you walk
Gently through the worlld
And know it's beauty
All the days of your life

(Esra Sloblock)

172.

Holding onto anger is like grasping a hot coal with the intent of throwing it at someone else, you are the one who gets burned.

(Buddha)

173.

Love is love's reward

(John Dryden)

174.

The most important thing a father can do for his children is to love their mother.

Theodore Hesburgh

175.

Happiness requires something to do, something to love and something to hope for.

(Swahili Proverb)

176.

Nobody can do for little children what grandparents do. Grandparents sort of sprinkle stardust over the lives of little children.

(Alex Haley)

177.

Jesus told them, "You are going to have the light just a little while longer. Walk while you have the light, before darkness overtakes you. Whoever walks in the dark does not know where they are going. Believe in the light while you have the light, so that you may become children of light." When he had finished speaking, Jesus left and hid himself from them.

(John 12: 35 -36)

178.

They Say There Is A Reason (Poem)

They say there is a reason,
They say that time will heal,
But neither time nor reason,
Will change the way I feel,
For no-one knows the heartache,
That lies behind our smiles,
No-one knows how many times,
We have broken down and cried,
We want to tell you something,
So there won't be any doubt,
You're so wonderful to think of,
But so hard to be without.

(Unknown)

179.

Disappointment is the nurse of wisdom.

(Sir Bayle Roche)

180.

It's sad when someone you know becomes someone you knew.

(Henry Rollins)

181.

Our dead are never dead to us, until we have forgotten them.

(George Eliot)

182.

Hurt

What have I become?
My sweetest friend
Everyone I know
Goes away in the end
You could have it all
My empire of dirt
I will let you down
I will make you hurt
If I could start again
A million miles away
I would keep myself
I would find a way

(Johnny Cash)

183.

Mothers hold their children's hands for a short while, but their hearts forever.

(Unknown)

184.

Sometimes when you lose your way, you find YOURSELF.

(Mandy Hale)

185.

Within the covers of the Bible are the answers for all the problems men face.

(Ronald Reagan)

186.

Smile, it's free therapy.

(Douglas Horton)

187.

I don't want my life to be defined by what is etched on a tombstone. I want it to be defined by what is etched in the lives and hearts of those I've touched.

(Steve Maraboli)

188.

We feel most alive when we are closest to death.

(Nenia Campbell)

189.

I believe in everything until it's disproved. So I believe in fairies, the myths, dragons. It all exists, even if it's in your mind. Who's to say that dreams and nightmares aren't as real as the here and now?

(John Lennon)

190.

God will not look you over for medals, degrees or diplomas but for scars.

(Elbert Hubbard)

191.

I was born the day you kissed me,
died the day you left me,
but lived for the time that you loved me"

(anju)

192.

A dream that is not interpreted
is like a letter that is unread.

(Jewish Proverb)

193.

How happy I was if I could forget
To remember how sad I am
Would be an easy adversity
But the recollecting of Bloom

Keeps making November difficult
Till I who was almost bold
Lose my way like a little Child
And perish of the cold.

(Emily Dickinson)

194.

If you can make it through the night, there's a brighter day.

(Tupac Shakur)

195.

When wealth is lost, nothing is lost; when health is lost, something is lost; when character is lost, all is lost.

(Billy Graham)

196.

Maybe all one can do is hope to end up with the right regrets.

(Arthur Miller)

197.

Treasure your relationships, not your possessions.

(J. D'Angelo)

198.

Behind the cloud the sun is still shining.

(Abraham Lincoln)

199.

If my ship sails from sight, it doesn't mean my journey ends, it simply means the river bends.

(Enoch Powell)

200.

You can love someone so much...But you can never love people as much as you can miss them.

(John Green)

201.

The darker the night, the brighter the stars, The deeper the grief, the closer is God!

(Fyodor Dostoevsky)

202.

Every day may not be good... but there's something good in every day

(Alice Morse Earle)

203.

Humor is one of the best ingredients of survival.

(Aung San Suu Kyi)

204.

Love is Immortal
Life is eternal,
and love is immortal,
and death is only a horizon;
and a horizon is nothing
save the limit of our sight.

(Rossiter Worthington Raymond)

205.

I look at life as a gift of God.
Now that he wants it back
I have no right to complain.

(Joyce Carey)

206.

Death leaves a heartache
no one can heal,
love leaves a memory
no one can steal

(Unknown)

207.

If I had a single flower
for every time I think about you,
I could walk forever in my garden.

(Claudia Ghandi)

208.

You never know how strong you are, until being
strong is your only choice.

(Bob Marley)

209.

Worrying about the world is a darkness in the heart,
while worrying about the Hereafter is a light
in the heart.

(Islamic Proverb)

210.

You'll Never Walk Alone

When you walk through a storm
Hold your head up high
And don't be afraid of the dark

At the end of a storm
There's a golden sky
And the sweet silver song of a lark

Walk on through the wind
Walk on through the rain
Though your dreams be tossed and blown

Walk on, walk on
With hope in your heart
And you'll never walk alone

You'll never walk alone

Walk on, walk on
With hope in your heart
And you'll never walk alone

You'll never walk alone.

(Gerry and the Pacemakers)

211.

No one is useless in this world who lightens the burden of it to anyone else.

(Charles Dickens)

212.

There are far, far better things ahead than any we leave behind.

(C. S. Lewis)

213.

I believe that everything happens for a reason. People change so that you can learn to let go, things go wrong so that you appreciate them when they're right, you believe lies so you eventually learn to trust no one but yourself, and sometimes good things fall apart so better things can fall together.

(Marilyn Monroe)

214.

I never feel lonely if I've got a book - they're like old friends. Even if you're not reading them over and over again, you know they are there. And they're part of your history. They sort of tell a story about your journey through life.

(Emilia Fox)

215.

It's funny how, when things seem the darkest, moments of beauty present themselves in the most unexpected places.

(Karen Marie Moning)

216.

Some roses grow through concrete. Remember that.

(Brandi L. Bates)

217.

God has put within our lives meanings and possibilities that quite outrun the limits of mortality.

(Harry Emerson Fosdick)

218.

Happiness is an inside job.

(William Arthur Ward)

219.

The power of imagination makes us infinite.

(John Muir)

220.

No man steps in the same river twice, for it's not the same river and he's not the same man.

(Heraclitus)

221.

Whoever lets himself be led by the heart will never lose his way

(Egyptian Proverb)

222.

The time you feel lonely is the time you most need to be by yourself.

(Douglas Coupland)

223.

Verses from: All Things Bright and Beautiful

All things bright and beautiful,
All creatures great and small,
All things wise and wonderful,
The Lord God made them all.

Each little flower that opens,
Each little bird that sings,
He made their glowing colours,
He made their tiny wings.

All things bright and beautiful,
All creatures great and small,
All things wise and wonderful,
The Lord God made them all.

The purple-headed mountain,
The river running by,
The sunset and the morning,
That brightens up the sky.

(William Henry Monk)

224.

Prayer should be the key of the day and the lock of the night.

(George Herbert)

225.

Grief is the price we pay for love.

(Queen Elizabeth II)

226.

A sympathetic friend can be quite as dear as a brother.

(Homer)

227.

When you arise in the morning, think of what a precious privilege it is to be alive - to breathe, to think, to enjoy, to love.

(Marcus Aurelius)

228.

Not forgiving someone is like not pulling a thorn out of your foot just because you weren't the one to put it there.

(Mercedes Lackey)

229.

Trying to forget someone you love is like trying to remember someone you never knew.

(Unknown)

230.

For I am already being poured out like a drink offering, and the time for my departure is near. I have fought the good fight, I have finished the race, I have kept the faith. Now there is in store for me the crown of righteousness, which the Lord, the righteous Judge, will award to me on that day—and not only to me, but also to all who have longed for his appearing.

(Timothy 4:6-9)

231.

Realize that if a door closed, it's because what was behind it wasn't meant for you.

(Mandy Hale)

232.

Only the young die good.

(Oliver Herford)

233.

Death smiles at us all, all a man can do is smile back.

(Marcus Aurelius)

234.

The important thing is not to stop questioning. Curiosity has its own reason for existing. One cannot help but be in awe when he contemplates the mysteries of eternity, of life, of the marvelous structure of reality. It is enough if one tries merely to comprehend a little of this mystery every day. Never lose a holy curiosity.

(Albert Einstein)

235.

And ever has it been known that love knows not its own depth until the hour of separation.

(Khalil Gibran)

236.

It's true we don't know what we've got until its gone, but we don't know what we've been missing until it arrives. Pleasure of love lasts but a moment, Pain of love lasts a lifetime.

(Bette Davis)

237.

Anyone who believes has eternal life.

(John 6:47)

238.

Heaven is a wonderful place and the benefits for the believer are out of this world.

(Billy Graham)

239.

No one wants to die. Even people who want to go to heaven don't want to die to get there. And yet, death is the destination we all share. No one has ever escaped it, and that is how it should be, because death is very likely the single best invention of life. It's life's change agent. It clears out the old to make way for the new.

(Steve Jobs)

240.

Happiness comes from striving to make tomorrow better than today and being at peace when yesterday was better than today as well.

(Dan Pearce)

241.

Life is too short to live the same day twice. So each new day make sure you live your life.

(Machine Gun Kelly)

242.

More than that, we rejoice in our sufferings, knowing that suffering produces endurance, and endurance produces character, and character produces hope, and hope does not put us to shame, because God's love has been poured into our hearts through the Holy Spirit who has been given to us.

(Romans 5:3-5)

243.

I believe in Islam. I am a Muslim and there is nothing wrong with being a Muslim, nothing wrong with the religion of Islam. It just teaches us to believe in Allah as the God. Those of you who are Christian probably believe in the same God, because I think you believe in the God Who created the universe. That's the One we believe in, the One Who created universe - the only difference being you call Him God and we call Him Allah. The Jews call Him Jehovah. If you could understand Hebrew, you would probably call Him Jehovah too. If you could understand Arabic, you would probably call Him Allah.

(Malcolm X)

244.

When you get older, it feels like happy memories and sad memories are pretty much the same thing. It is all just emotion in the end. And any of it can make you weep.

(Nick Hornby)

245.

In Life, We never Lose Friends, We Only Learn Who Our True Ones Are

(Unknown)

246.

Compassion is an action word with no boundaries.

(Prince)

247.

How far you go in life depends on your being tender with the young, compassionate with the aged, sympathetic with the striving and tolerant of the weak and strong. Because someday in your life you will have been all of these.

(George Washington)

248.

One never knows the ending. One has to die to know exactly what happens after death, although Catholics have their hopes.

(Alfred Hitchcock)

249.

Only put off until tomorrow what you are willing to die having left undone.

(Pablo Picasso)

250.

To die will be an awfully big adventure.

(J.M. Barrie)

251.

Sometimes the only way the good Lord can get into some hearts is to break them.

(Fulton J. Sheen)

252.

Daffodils by William Wordsworth

I wander'd lonely as a cloud
That floats on high o'er vales and hills,
When all at once I saw a crowd,
A host of golden daffodils,
Beside the lake, beneath the trees
Fluttering and dancing in the breeze.

Continuous as the stars that shine
And twinkle on the milky way,
They stretch'd in never-ending line
Along the margin of a bay:
Ten thousand saw I at a glance
Tossing their heads in sprightly dance.

The waves beside them danced, but they
Out-did the sparkling waves in glee: -
A poet could not but be gay
In such a jocund company!
I gazed - and gazed - but little thought
What wealth the show to me had brought.

For oft, when on my couch I lie
In vacant or in pensive mood,
They flash upon that inward eye
Which is the bliss of solitude;
And then my heart with pleasure fills
And dances with the daffodils.

253.

Stop holding on to the person
Who has let go of you.
Move on.

(Trent Shelton)

254.

Since God intends to make you like Jesus, he will take you through the same experiences Jesus went through. That includes loneliness, temptation, stress, criticism, rejection, and many other problems.

(Rick Warren)

255.

There isn't a tree in the world that the
wind hasn't shaken.

(Hindu Proverb)

256.

The important thing is that when your come to understand something you act on it, no matter how small that act is. Eventually it will take you where you need to go.

(Helen Prejean)

257.

I don't pay attention to the
world ending.
it has ended for me
many times
and began again in the morning.

(Nayyirah Waheed)

258.

Death ends a life, not a relationship.
(Mitch Albom)

259.

Yesterday is history, tomorrow is a mystery, today is a gift of God, which is why we call it the present.
(Bill Keane)

260.

Life's under no obligation to give us what we expect.
(Margaret Mitchell)

261.

Blessed is he who expects nothing, for he shall never be disappointed.

(Alexander Pope)

262.

You can cut all the flowers but you cannot keep Spring from coming.

(Pablo Neruda)

263.

We are all connected; to each other, biologically. To the earth, chemically. To the rest of the universe atomically.

(Neil DeGrasse Tyson)

264.

Rejection is an opportunity for your selection.

(Bernard Branson)

265.

You were born a child of light's wonderful secret— you return to the beauty you have always been.

(Aberjhani)

266.

Leave the door open for the unknown, the door into the dark. That's where the most important things come from, where you yourself came from, and where you will go.

(Rebecca Solnit)

267.

The most painful thing is losing yourself in the process of loving someone too much, and forgetting that you are special too.

(Ernest Hemingway)

268.

Unfortunately, the clock is ticking, the hours are going by. The past increases, the future recedes. Possibilities decreasing, regrets mounting.

(Haruki Murakami)

269.

We were together. I forget the rest.

(Walt Whitman)

270.

Let nothing disturb you,
Let nothing frighten you,
All things are passing away:
God never changes.
Patience obtains all things.
Whoever has God lacks nothing;
God alone suffices.
(Santa Teresa de Jesús)

271.

You are loved more than you will ever know by someone who died to know you.

(Romans 5:8)

272.

The best way to find yourself is to lose yourself in the service of others.

(Mahatma Ghandi)

273.

Now at last they were beginning Chapter One of the Great Story no one on earth has ever read, which goes on forever; in which every chapter is better than the one before.

(C.S Lewis)

274.

Together in Electric Dreams

I only knew you for a while
I never saw your smile
'Til it was time to go
Time to go away (time to go away)
Sometimes it's hard to recognise
Love comes as a surprise
And it's too late
It's just too late to stay
Too late to stay.

We'll always be together
However far it seems (love never ends).
We'll always be together
Together in electric dreams.

(Giorgio Moroder, Philip Oakey)

275.

Just always be waiting for me.

(J.M.Barrie - Peter Pan)

276.

But Not Forgotten

I think no matter where you stray,
That I shall go with you a way.
Though you may wander sweeter lands,
You will not forget my hands,
Nor yet the way I held my head
Nor the tremulous things I said.
You will still see me, small and white
And smiling, in the secret night,
And feel my arms about you when
The day comes fluttering back again.
I think, no matter where you be,
You'll hold me in your memory
And keep my image there without me,
By telling later loves about me.

(Dorothy Parker)

277.

Go where your best prayers take you.

(Frederick Buechner)

278.

Dying is one thing to be sad over...Living unhappily is something else

(Morrie Schwartz)

279.

The most beautiful people we have known are those who have known defeat, known suffering, known struggle, known loss, and have found their way out of the depths.

(Elisabeth Kübler-Ross)

280.

Just think of all the people that you knew in the past
that passed on, they in heaven, found peace at last
Picture a place that they exist, together
There has to be a place better than this, in Heaven

(Tupac Shakur)

281.

Visualize this thing that you want, see it, feel it, believe in it. Make your mental blue print, and begin to build.

(Robert Collier)

282.

Do not fear what you are about to suffer. Behold, the devil is about to throw some of you into prison, that you may be tested, and for ten days you will have tribulation. Be faithful unto death, and I will give you the crown of life.

(Revelation 2:10)

283.

Fervent prayers produce phenomenal results.

(Woodrow Kroll)

284.

Carry On

Walking alone and the shores are longing
I miss your footprints next to mine
Sure as the waves on the sands are washing
Your rhythm keeps my heart in time

You, you found me
Made me into something new
Led me through the deepest waters
I promise loud to carry on for you

(Rita Ora/Kygo)

285.

Faith has to do with things that are not seen and hope with things that are not at hand.

(Thomas Aquinas)

286.

Then stirs the feeling infinite, so felt In solitude, where we are least alone.

(Lord Byron)

287.

Lying in my bed I hear the clock tick
And think of you
Caught up in circles
Confusion is nothing new
Flashback, warm nights
Almost left behind
Suitcases of memories
Time after.

(Cyndi Lauper- Time after Time)

288.

Somewhere in time's own space, there must be some sweet, pastured place
Where creeks sing on - and tall trees grow, some paradise where horses go,
For by the love that guides my pen, I know great horses live again.

(Stanley Harrison)

289.

We can never obtain peace in the outer world until we make peace with ourselves.

(Dalai Lama)

290.

Tears are God's gift to us. Our holy water.
They heal us as they flow.

(Rita Schiano)

291.

It is thought and feeling which guides the
universe, not deeds.

(Edgar Cayce)

292.

Life always offers you a second chance.
is called tomorrow.

(Dylan Thomas)

293.

To see a world in a grain of sand
And a heaven in a wild flower,
Hold infinity in the palm of your hand,
And eternity in an hour.

(William Blake)

294.

You know it's love when all you want is that person to be happy, even if you're not part of their happiness.

(Julia Roberts)

295.

Life is like an ever-shifting kaleidoscope - a slight change, and all patterns alter.

(Sharon Salzberg)

296.

Your life does not get better by chance, it gets better by change.

(Jim Rohn)

297.

Reincarnation makes life what it is intended to be a glorious adventure in which victory is absolutely sure to be ours if we persist. It proves that man [is] ... master of his fate on his road to the stars.

(Shaw Desmond)

298.

Go within every day and find the inner strength so that the world will not Blow your candle out.

(Katherine Dunham)

299.

It lies not in our power to love, or hate, For will in us is over-rul'd by fate.

(Christopher Marlowe)

300.

I pray to God to remove my enemies from my life, and before I know it I started losing friends. Am just saying no one to be trusted.

(Blaze Olamiday)

301.

Heaven wheels above you, displaying to you her eternal glories, and still your eyes are on the ground.

(Dante Alighieri)

302.

It hurts to have someone in your heart that you can't have in your arms.

(Unknown)

303.

Treasured memories of days gone by.

(S.D Harrazie)

304.

Regrets only apply when we don't learn from a situation. No sense looking back, look forward with new knowledge and no regret.

(Catherine Pulsifer)

305.

Don't grieve. Anything you lose comes round in another form.

(Rumi)

306.
My Way

And now, the end is here
And so I face the final curtain
My friend, I'll say it clear
I'll state my case, of which I'm certain
I've lived a life that's full
I traveled each and ev'ry highway
And more, much more than this, I did it my way

Regrets, I've had a few
But then again, too few to mention
I did what I had to do and saw it through without exemption
I planned each charted course, each careful step along the byway
And more, much more than this, I did it my way

Yes, there were times, I'm sure you knew
When I bit off more than I could chew
But through it all, when there was doubt
I ate it up and spit it out
I faced it all and I stood tall and did it my way

I've loved, I've laughed and cried
I've had my fill, my share of losing
And now, as tears subside, I find it all so amusing
To think I did all that
And may I say, not in a shy way,
"Oh, no, oh, no, not me, I did it my way"

For what is a man, what has he got?
If not himself, then he has naught
To say the things he truly feels and not the words of one who kneels
The record shows I took the blows and did it my way!

Yes, it was my way

(P. Anka, J. Revaux, G. Thibault, C. Frankois)

307.

Sweet is the memory of a distant friend! Like the mellow rays of the departing sun, it falls tenderly, yet sadly, on the heart.

(Washington Irving)

308.

All that they were

All the world's a stage,

And all the men and women merely players:

They have their exits and their entrances;

And one man in his time plays many parts.

(William Shakepeare)

309.

The broken heart. You think you will die, but you keep living, day after day after terrible day.

(Charles Dickens)

310.

We must remember that the shortest distance between our problems and their solutions is the distance between our knees and the floor.

(Charles Stanley)

311.

That's how you know you love someone, I guess, when you can't experience anything without wishing the other person were there to see it, too.

(Kaui Hart Hemmings)

312.

We're all expendable. We think the world's going to stop when a pope dies, or a king. And then... life goes on.

(Sylvester Stallone)

313.

If you love someone, set them free. If they come back they're yours; if they don't they never were.

(Richard Bach)

314.

Someday, everything will make perfect sense. So for now, laugh at the confusion, smile through the tears, be strong and keep reminding yourself that everything happens for a reason.

(John Mayer)

315.

I will walk by faith, even when I cannot see.

(Jeremy Camp)

316.

Some days, 24 hours is too much to stay put in, so I take the day hour by hour, moment by moment. I break the task, the challenge, the fear into small, bite-size pieces. I can handle a piece of fear, depression, anger, pain, sadness, loneliness, illness. I actually put my hands up to my face, one next to each eye, like blinders on a horse.

(Regina Brett)

317.

In the middle of my little mess, I forget how BIG I'm blessed!

(Francesca Battistelli)

318.

Five daily Reminders 1. You only fail if you quit. 2. Everyone's journey is different. 3. Things always get better with time. 4. The past cannot be changed. 5. Happiness is found within.

(Unknown)

319.

Take pride in how far you have come & have faith in how far you can go.

(Anil Kumar Sinha)

320.

Flatter me, and I may not believe you. Criticize me, and I may not like you. Ignore me, and I may not forgive you. Encourage me, and I will not forget you. Love me and I may be forced to love you."

(William Arthur Ward)

321.

Indeed we belong to Allah, and indeed to him we will return.

(Quran 2:156)

322.

Words can never adequately convey the incredible impact of our attitudes toward life. The longer I live the more convinced I become that life is 10 percent what happens to us and 90 percent how we respond to it.

(Chuck Swindoll)

323.

I just find myself happy with the simple things. Appreciating the blessings God gave me.

(DMX)

324.

It doesn't matter who likes you or who doesn't like you, all that matters is God likes you. He accepts you, he approves of you

(Joel Osteen)

325.

One day you'll leave this world behind, so live a life you will remember.

(Avicii)

326.

Pray for someone else's child, your pastor, the military, the police officers, the firemen, the teachers, the government. There's no end to the ways that you can intervene on behalf of others through prayer.

(Monica Johnson)

327.

His Journey's Just Begun

Don't think of him as gone away
his journey's just begun,
life holds so many facets
this earth is only one.
Just think of him as resting
from the sorrows and the tears
in a place of warmth and comfort
where there are no days and years.
Think how he must be wishing
that we could know today
how nothing but our sadness
can really pass away.
And think of him as living
in the hearts of those he touched...
for nothing loved is ever lost
and he was loved so much.

(Ellen Brenneman)

328.

I do not fear death.
I had been dead for billions and billions
of years before I was born,
and had not suffered the slightest inconvenience from it.
(Mark Twain)

329.

If Only I Knew

If only I knew that our time would be so brief,
Spoiled you rotten I would have done.
If only I knew that would be our last phone call,
Just to listen to you speak, held on longer I would have done.
If only I knew that would be your last text,
Kept it in my inbox I would have done.

If only I knew it was the last time I was seeing you,
Called you back and hugged you tight I would have done.
If only I knew it was the last time I would see you smile,
Stood longer and watch you smile I would have done.
If only I knew that I was seeing your face for the last time,
Memorize all its features I would have done.

If only I knew that God would take you away so soon,
Spend all my time with you I would have done.
There are a lot of things I would have done differently
If only I had known.

(Sennette Gaoses)

330.

Dating an ex is the equivalent of failing a test you already have the answers to.

(Kendrick Cole)

331.

Not without hope we suffer and we mourn.

(William Wordsworth)

332.

Forgiving another does not erase bitter past memories. Changing that memory through healing is our only hope for a positive future. Remember, though - a healed memory is not a deleted memory. One will always remember and never forget.

(William E Lewis Jr)

333.

Promise me, you won't forget our laughs, our jokes, our smiles, our conversations, our plans, our tears, our memories, our experiences, our friendships.

(Unknown)

334.

Maybe life isn't about avoiding the bruises. Maybe its about collecting the scars to prove that we showed up.

(Hannah Brencher)

335.

Angels In The Stars

God saw I was getting tired
as he put his arms around me,
as he whispered come with me.

There is a place for you in heaven
where there is no suffering and no pain.
All you have to do is look up to the sky
and know that you will see me.

As I am an angel in the stars,
what a great place to be.
I am an angel of God, and a
sparkle I shall be.

Know that I'm watching over you;
just look up and see.
I'm looking, watching over you.
Please don't be sad for me.

I'm your angel in the stars
where I am happy now.
You will see and one day
you will be with me.

(Sara Manis)

336.

Where is love there is life.

(Mahatma Gandhi)

337.

When I got untethered from the comfort of religion, it wasn't a loss of faith for me, it was a discovery of self...had faith that I'm capable enough to handle any situation. There's peace in understanding that I have only one life, here and now, and I'm responsible.

(Brad Pitt)

338.

We don't develop courage by being happy every day. We develop it by surviving difficult times and challenging adversity.

(Barbara de Angelis)

339.

A Sunrise is God's way of saying, Let's start again.

(Todd Stocker)

340.

Come back. Even as a shadow, even a dream.

(Euripides)

341.

Do not bring people in your life who weigh you down, and trust your instincts. Good relationships feel good. They feel right. They don't hurt. They're not painful. That's not just with somebody you want to marry, but it's with the friends you choose. It's with the people you surround yourself with.

(Michelle Obama)

342

Spirit In The Sky

Prepare yourself you know it's a must
Gotta have a friend in Jesus
So you know that when you die
He's gonna recommend you
To the spirit in the sky
Gonna recommend you
To the spirit in the sky
That's where you're gonna go when you die
When you die and they lay you to rest
You're gonna go to the place that's the best

(Norman Greenbaum)

343.

Never regret yesterday. Life is in you today and you make your tomorrow.

(L. Ron Hubbard)

344.

If you're going through hell, keep going.

(Winston Churchill)

345.

More tears are shed over answered prayers than unanswered ones.

(Mother Theresa)

346.

Before you diagnose yourself with depression or low self-esteem, first make sure you are not, in fact, surrounded by assholes.

(Sigmund Freud)

347.

It is prosperity that gives us friends, adversity that proves them.

(Romanian Proverbs)

348.

I Will Always Love You

If I should stay
I would only be in your way
So, I'll go but I know
I'll think of you
Each step of the way

And I will always love you
And I will always love you

Bittersweet memories
That is all I am taking with me
So goodbye, please don't you cry
'Cause we both know I'm not what you need
And I will always love you
I will always love you

I hope life treats you kind
And I hope you have all you've dreamed of
I wish you joy and happiness
But above all, I wish you love

And I will always love you
And I will always love you
And I will always love you

(Dolly Parton)

349.

For me, singing sad songs often has a way of healing a situation. It gets the hurt out in the open into the light, out of the darkness.

(Reba McEntire)

350.

Love is something eternal; the aspect may change, but not the essence.

(Vincent Van Gogh)

351.

When we pray we speak to God; but when we read, God speaks to us.

(Saint Jerome)

352.

All I have seen teaches me to trust the creator for all I have not seen.

(Ralph Waldo Emerson)

353.

I have noticed even people who claim everything is predestined, and that we can do nothing to change it, look before they cross the road.

(Stephen Hawking)

354.

Even if I go through the deepest darkness,
I will not be afraid, Lord,
for you are with me.
Your shepherd's rod and staff protect me.

(Psalm 23:4)

355.

Shared misfortune, less sorrow.

(Spanish Proverb)

356.

It's a funny old world - a man's lucky if
he gets out of it alive.

(W.C. Fields)

357.

Fire is the test of gold; adversity, of strong men.
(Martha Graham)

358.

Kids go where there is excitement. They stay where there is love.
(Zig Ziglar)

359.

Self-care is never a selfish act—it is simply good stewardship of the only gift I have, the gift I was put on earth to offer to others."
(Parker Palmer)

360.

Low self-esteem is like driving through life with your hand-break on.
(Maxwell Maltz)

361.

If we remembered everyday that we could lose someone at any moment, we would love them more fiercely and freely and without fear – not because there is nothing to lose, but because everything can always be lost.
(Emily Rapp)

362.

Our ultimate finishing line in life is death! Whilst you have life, work hard and trust God!

(Ernest Agyemang Yeboah)

363.

There is no key to happiness; the door is always open.

(Mother Teresa)

364.

Sometimes, when we reach for the stars, we fall short. But we must pick ourselves up again and press on despite the pain.

(Ronald Reagan)

365.

Grief O Master, Master of Grief

As the tears run down my face, I realise
your gone forever, Grief O Master.

The Numbness, the knotting of my stomach,
for I have no appetite, Grief O Master.

The sun shines bright, the birds sing, children laugh,
but I cannot hear, Grief O Master.

Every moments of each day are a painful reminder
that I will never see you again, Grief O Master.

Grief you are my Master and I am your servant,
Grief O Master.

My new life of solitude and battling thoughts of
the What ifs and the What Might have been,
Grief O Master.

A life in servitude, a life of torture, agony,
there's no way back, Grief O Master.

Then one-day out of the abyss, I heard
you call my Name.

A message sent to reclaim me from my Master.

Yes! I remember you had never left me, you
have always been here, your physical presence
is no more, but I can think of you at any-time,
and your always in my heart.

Now each day I feel the sun, the wind and rain,
I enjoy the laugher of children and the sounds
of the birds singing.

I gladly remember our time together and
you will always be with me, the pain is no more.

This is what you wanted.

I am Master of Grief.

(S.D Harrazie)

Afterword

It has been an incredible and emotional experience writing this book; The book took me around 5 months to research, write, format and edit. But I have carefully curated some of the Worlds most ancient passages and versus alongside more contemporary examples. The idea of this was I wanted to produce a compilation of uplifting sayings and quotes, prayers and songs that people right across the four corners of globe could directly relate to. This would be key to getting the reader to unlock their most positive thoughts, memories and beliefs.

Nobody knows exactly when grief and loss will interrupt their lives, and in that sense I am no different to anyone else. I suppose I will never forget the experience of writing this book. My World at the start of writing this book would be a very different World to the one - when I had completed the book. As I sat at my desk looking through a book of Psalms and listening to the Radio, I heard a song play on the Radio. "Wow" I thought I really liked a particular chorus in the song - as I pondered putting it in this book. I was unsure who actually sang the song and what the song was about? Just at this precise moment I had a call from my mother. She told me she had some bad news for me - my Father had died after an illness in hospital. I was not particularly close to my Father as he lived in a different part of the Country, and my parents had divorced when I was an infant, nevertheless still very bad news for everyone all round.

A few weeks later went by and I went back to where I left off on the book, point 47 (Blank space), then I remembered the catchy chorus that I had thought about including; before I was interrupted with the terrible news. Hmm I need to investigate this.. and include the verse. I'd like to think that this was message sent to me by my late father.

Anyhow I know lots and lots of readers will have plenty of similar stories of songs, prayers and verses that totally describe their experience of grief and loss. So this book is especially for YOU - to bring you a positive message that everything is going to be just fine.

This is second book in the **Motivation 365 series**, so please look out for my other books that are aimed at self-help and improvement in specialised areas of life.

Lastly………….

If you liked this book or found it useful, I would be extremely grateful if you could leave a short review on Amazon. Your support means a great deal and does make a difference. I personally read all reviews and I'm constantly seeking improvement and welcome feedback.

Thanks again for your support.